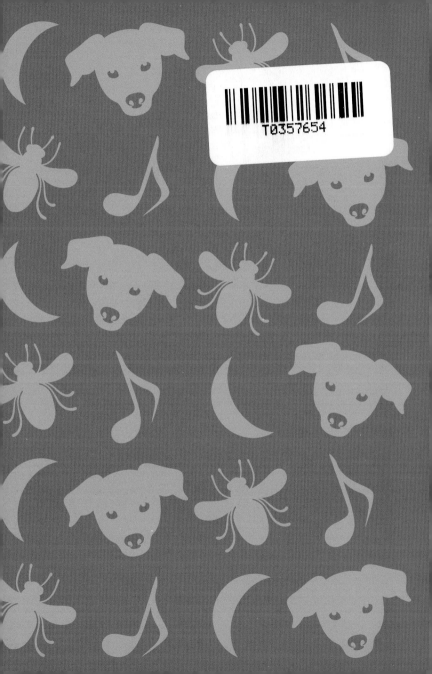

BE MORE
ARIANA

CONTENTS

INTRODUCTION

From the moment she struts into your life, it's impossible to forget Ariana Grande. No one sings like Ari—her once-in-a-generation high notes take us to the clouds. But despite her angelic pipes and tiny stature, she's no featherweight as a popstar. She brings a twisted sense of humor and playful sexiness to her performances which set her apart. The relatability of her songs maintain her connection to her fans: that's always going to be our Ari, who we watched grow from a baby popstar to a world-conquering hero.

She's also renowned for her kindness and authenticity. Over the course of her career, Ariana has been to darker places than she could ever have expected, and somehow found her way back to the light. Personal losses and public scandals have brought out the true Ariana for all the world to see: wounded and vulnerable, but also strong and compassionate. She teaches us how to be kind and open, but also how to stick up for ourselves in this world and how to do it all with a sense of humor.

Tie that ponytail a little higher, step into her stiletto boots, and discover 25 ways to be more Ariana.

CHAPTER 1

THERE'S ONLY

ONE ARIANA

Being told to "Be yourself" sounds cringe when you first hear it. No, I want to be someone shinier and brighter than that! But it's actually the best advice you'll ever get. Look at Ariana. It's the unique, quirkier parts of her that add salt to her popstar sweetener and make her such an intriguing, enduring artist.

"I'm a huge advocate of self-expression, being yourself, and encouraging people to embrace who they are…"

YOU'VE GOT TO BE YOU

Ariana Grande started her career on the Nickelodeon, in shows like *Sam & Cat*. Working on a TV set was great training, but it wouldn't be long before she wanted to grow beyond her child star image. Her first ever hit, "Put Your Hearts Up", was a moment of clarity for the 18-year-old Ariana: "It was geared toward kids and felt so inauthentic and fake. For the video, they gave me a bad spray tan and put me in a princess dress and had me frolic around the street". Ariana's career changed when she embraced her authentic self. Evolving into a more soulful, grownup singer on songs like "Dangerous Woman", she eventually took the greatest chance of all. Recorded in just two weeks, the album *Thank U, Next* changed the game for Ari and for pop in general. It was straight from the heart but natural, like a conversation with your funniest friend, if they had a four-octave range. Being herself was a risk but look how much it paid off!

"I'm super girly when it comes to fashion,
but on the inside I'm only fascinated with
dark, macabre, and weird things."

EMBRACE YOUR WEIRD

Ariana is at once the cutest girly-girl to ever rock a bow, and also part goth and horror-movie enthusiast. Her house is decorated for Hallowe'en all year round and she used to keep a folder of screenshots of demons. But at the same time, she takes a sunshine attitude to life and brings so much light to anyone who hears her spectacular, airy singing.

So, what gives?

Because of her perky ponytail and doll-like appearance, the public often expect Ariana to be like the stereotypical girl (remember when a DJ asked her whether she could possibly choose between makeup and her phone?). But, like all of us, Ari is more than how she looks on the outside. Our particular tastes make us who we are, no matter how unusual they are.

Embracing her contrasts means there's always more to learn about Ariana.

"You should feel grateful and happy that you're healthy, you're alive, and that you are loved... Whatever weight you are, whatever situation you're in, whether you have a breakout, whatever it is—you are loved."

YOUR BODY, YOUR BUSINESS

Women in the public eye get so much negative attention that sometimes not even fan love can outweigh it. Despite being one of the most charismatic and talented people in the world, Ariana still gets endless comments about her looks.

It's not okay to shame celebrities for their bodies. But they're not the only ones who are held to impossible standards—out in the wider world, girls, women, and increasingly men everywhere are constantly being given the message that their bodies should look different.

How about, as Ariana suggests, we accept there is more than one way to be beautiful and limit ourselves to comments that are kind? If we required everyone to look like a supermodel, 5ft-tall Ari wouldn't be considered gorgeous. When you look at it that way, it's just ridiculous.

"I'm [...] going to be a human being who cares about other human beings; to be an ally and use my privilege to help educate people."

TREASURE YOUR INTEGRITY

Ariana's fans are united by a love of joyful pop songs that
are somehow always the right thing for the right moment.
That doesn't mean we'll all hold the same opinions on current
affairs. So, when she speaks her mind about issues such as
which way to vote, she does it knowing she'll get backlash:
"There's a lot of noise when you say anything about anything."
We've all been there, wondering if we're "allowed" to say what
we think, especially if we feel people around us will shame
us for our opinions. Ariana *knows* people will disagree with her,
and she does it anyway. She has spoken out on gun control,
LGBTQ+ rights, and Black Lives Matter, making it clear that she
understands this could damage her career: "I would rather
sell fewer records and be outspoken about what I think [...] than
sell more records." That's the thing about integrity—Ariana
knows she might lose money and fame from her stances,
but she accepts that as the price of doing what's right.

"

I have [an] idea of [...]
this stronger, amazing,
fearless version of
myself that one day
I hope to evolve into.
Sometimes I try to
be that for my fans
before I actually
am that myself.

"

BECOMING THE DIVA YOU WERE BORN TO BE

Ari is a dreamer. In the first track on *Thank U, Next*, "Imagine", she pictures a perfect life with her boyfriend. This daydreaming extends into every part of her life, including envisioning the person she wants to be: a confident woman who her fans can look up to. When she sang these words in 2019, Ariana had been working for over ten years and had grown up in the public eye. She understood that you can "fake it 'til you make it" when it comes to confidence. By walking tall and power-dressing, Ari owns every stage she struts onto, no matter what she's feeling inside. We can use Ariana's template for our own personal growth by writing down three words that define the person we would like to become. While we're on that journey, listening to Ariana's songs and copying her swagger can help you fake it 'til you make it too.

CHAPTER 2

HOW MUCH

TO GIVE

Being a kind and giving person is wonderful. Don't ever stop doing that. It makes the world a better place and it's part of Ariana's incredible creativity. But if you find yourself giving too much, take a breath. Ariana has worked out that she doesn't owe people her entire self, her every thought, or 100% of her energy.

"It's hard to sing songs that are about wounds that are so fresh. It's fun, it's pop music, and I'm not trying to make it sound like anything that it's not, but these songs to me really do represent some heavy ****."

GET YOUR FEELINGS DOWN QUICKLY

Unlike some musicians, Ariana doesn't spend years agonizing over every drum sound or note in her music. She prefers to go into the studio and quickly lay down what she's feeling right now in the moment. It's like the musical equivalent of journaling. It's great for fans because we get to hear about what she's going through at every stage of her life. It's also why Ariana is consistently one of the coolest popstars in the game: her music is the sound of right now. By not overthinking how she expresses herself, Ariana fights the anxiety that comes with trying to do things perfectly all the time. *Thank U, Next* was written and recorded in two weeks. It captured the whirlwind she had been through in the previous two years, with triumph and trauma, with love and loss, with public displays of affection and Pete Davidson. By simply saying just what she felt, she changed the music industry.

"Love comes in many different forms.
You can love somebody and not be in love with
them. They can break your heart and you can
cry over it but still not be in love with them.
Love is a really peculiar thing."

THANKS, BUT... NEXT!

The title track on *Thank U, Next* is its breeziest and yet most impactful song. Everyone expected it to be mean and bitter, but instead she took the high ground, thanking her exes for what they taught her about life and ending with a triumphant declaration of self-love. What the media called her "failed relationships" became Ari's greatest moment of success: the song was her first Billboard Hot 100 number one single. The video was a riot of references from her favorite movies such as *Mean Girls* and *Legally Blonde*. But the biggest takeaway was Ari's gracious and effervescently light attitude to the very different loves of her life. She can laugh about boyfriends who she kind of loved, ones she never really loved, and certain ones she will always love. On albums like *Eternal Sunshine*, we've seen this wise attitude continue. On songs like "bye", which seems to be about the end of her marriage, she "tried to make sure it was kind and giving credit for trying and for the goodness that there was."

"I want everyone to be my friend.
I desperately love and want to hug
everyone I encounter."

JUST WANTING TO BE LIKED

There's something in every popstar that drives them to give
sunshine and entertainment to everyone in the world. It's a
beautiful instinct. But for many celebrities, and many ordinary
people too, there comes a point where giving so much can
become draining. Have you ever been at a party, trying to be
the sparkliest version of yourself so everyone will like you?
Or worked so hard for your A-grade that you had nothing left
to give at the end of the day? It's exhausting. Rather than giving
101% to other people, think about toning it down a little.
You are enough as you are, whether other people respond to it
or not. The fact is, even Ariana has her haters. Not everyone is
going to like us, no matter how badly we want to be best friends
with that awesome girl we just met. It's honestly okay. You will
find the people who do want to be around you and, like Ari,
develop a set of friends who love you right back.

WOMEN'S RIGHTS ARE HUMAN RIGHTS

"I'll never be able to swallow the fact that people feel the need to attach a successful woman to a man when they say her name."

KNOW WHEN TO PUT YOUR FOOT DOWN

Despite some of her music being all breezy lightness, Ariana doesn't play "the cool girl" who never gets offended by anything. Instead, she speaks her mind about the double standards affecting women. Ariana has seen too many headlines defining a female celebrity as someone's ex. She realized it wasn't about her; it was a failure of the media and the way we talk about women in society as a whole. This can affect those of us who aren't in the public eye too. Being constantly asked if you are dating someone, or "why you're still single", or when you're getting married is a way of telling girls and women that we're not enough on our own. Ariana won't stand for this nonsense. In 2024, she noted that coverage of her personal life continued to overshadow her work: "This is what the tabloids do to people, especially women, based on whether or not we like the person."

66

I see [...] the whole judgmental world of pop culture waiting with their pitchforks and torches. At the end of the day I don't care what they have to say, but knowing that every little thing I do is documented is a lot of pressure.

99

RISE ABOVE IT

Ariana has experienced more than her fair share of criticism over the years. Some of these conversations have come from a genuine place, like concerns about cultural appropriation in Ariana's videos and overall appearance. Then there was the ridiculously overblown scandal over supposedly licking a doughnut in a café in 2015. Some people did not like Ari publicly criticising Donald Trump during the American election. A problem with modern internet culture is that it's hard to know what to think when every action receives a similar amount of backlash and snark, regardless of how harmful it really is. This can lead to ignoring every conversation because it's all just too overwhelming. Instead of ignoring a cacophony of opinions, we can rise above the pressure and make our own decisions, in line with our values. We all make mistakes, and they're increasingly captured on camera (or doughnut shop CCTV). All we can do is laugh and learn from our missteps in the future.

CHAPTER 3

NO TEARS LEFT

TO CRY

Ariana's had to face more heartbreak than most people, and she's done it in the public eye. By talking publicly about her struggles with grief and trauma, she's started a conversation about how to cope. She doesn't have the answers; no one does. But follow her example: keep talking and sharing what you're going through.

"The sense of community that I saw in response to what happened was the best example of humanity."

WHEN THE WORST HAPPENS

In 2017, the worst possible thing happened. A terrorist set off a bomb at Ariana's May 22 concert, just as fans were leaving the Manchester Arena after enjoying the show. Twenty-two people were killed and thousands more were injured and traumatized. In the aftermath, Ariana, her fans, and the people of Manchester were left reeling.

When something terrible happens to you, it's natural to want to find a safe space and protect yourself. A shaken and horrified Ariana flew home to her mother and her boyfriend. But she didn't forget that many people had been impacted more than she had. She sprang into action to arrange One Love Manchester, a huge benefit concert to raise money for the victims of the attack and to show the world that the forces of joy and unity couldn't be defeated.

"

You hear about these things. You see it on the news, you tweet the hashtag. [...] But experiencing something like that firsthand, you think of everything differently...

"

LET PEOPLE IN

When you lose a loved one, or experience a traumatic event, it changes you. Suddenly, you can't relate to your friends who haven't been through the same experiences. You might not get any pleasure from your old hobbies anymore and just want to hide away. These are the moments that can really change your life and make you see everything differently. If you're the person who has suffered the trauma, seek out others who can understand what you've been through—for example, in a support group or an online forum. But don't lose touch with your existing friends—they still love you, even if they're not sure how to support you. In the aftermath of the Manchester bombing, Ariana chose to let others help her. Her friends, like Miley Cyrus and Justin Bieber, turned up to support her when she needed it most.

"I thought with time, and therapy, and writing, and pouring my heart out, and talking to my friends and family that it would be easier to talk about, but it's still so hard to find the words."

IT'S OKAY NOT TO BE OKAY

A year after the bombing, Ariana told an interviewer that she hadn't "healed" or found any kind of easy relief from the horrible events in Manchester. Resisting the urge to make others feel better by performing closure, she instead said:

"I feel like I shouldn't even be talking about my own experience—like I shouldn't even say anything. I don't think I'll ever know how to talk about it and not cry."

It's admirable that Ari keeps the victims in her thoughts and doesn't focus on herself. In private, though, it's important to allow ourselves to experience our feelings and acknowledge that we have pain too. Some events are bigger than our ability to cope with them, and that's okay. Whatever you're going through, your feelings are valid even if you can't put them into words.

"When I got home from tour, I had really wild dizzy spells, this feeling like I couldn't breathe [...] There were a couple of months straight where I felt so upside down."

YOUR BODY KNOWS BEST

If you have symptoms like Ariana's, take a moment to breathe and notice what's going on. Do you feel dizzy, or does it hurt somewhere? Your body wants what's best for you, and it's sending you signals. Sometimes you need to rest, read a book, or have a cuddle. Sometimes you need to take action to remove the stressful thing that's hurting you, whether that's a toxic friendship or an obsessive scrolling habit. Of course, sometimes you can't do anything about the source of anxiety except take good care of yourself. Ari wrote a whole song about these sorts of feelings, "Get Well Soon". With lyrics about taking care of your body and being there for people, she explained: "It's just about being there for each other and helping each other through scary times and anxiety." It appeared on *Sweetener*, the first album she released after the bombing. Take a page out of Ariana's book: keep putting one foot in front of the other, give yourself time, and make sure to sing at the top of your lungs.

"Sometimes it's kind of just about being the light in a situation."

YOU CAN ONLY DO YOU

When you're in the midst of a traumatic event, everyone does the best they can. When the dust settles, you might wish you had done things differently, whether you were the victim of the trauma or someone who tried to help. Try not to beat yourself up over "what might have been". Everyone is a beginner at life and there's no perfect way to handle its ups and downs. Ariana took advice from the mother of the bombing victim Olivia Campbell-Hardy: "play the hits and sing your heart out". This inspired her to help by doing what she does best. A stressful time does not magically change you into a different person with different skills. When it comes to helping others, try the Ariana method. If you are a good listener, use that skill. If you're better at doing practical things, offer that kind of help. Ari was able to arrange One Love Manchester, visit victims in hospital, and donate money and gifts.

CHAPTER 4

DANGEROUS

WOMAN

Ariana is a true diva: powerful, vulnerable, and unafraid to share her talent. In a world that wants you to be smaller and quieter, Ariana shows that we can use our voice, both onstage and out in the world. Take this tip from Ari: live your life so fully and authentically you that a drag queen could one day perform a tribute to you.

"I like having my funny character that I play
that feels like this exaggerated version of myself.
It protects me... If drag queens can dress up
as me, then I'm a character."

DON'T BE AFRAID TO BE BIG

Imagine you're Ariana, just about to step out onstage. The ponytail is high, the microphone is on, and the crowd is chanting your name. Your job is to go out there and sparkle as hard as you can for the fans. You wouldn't tell yourself to "tone it down", would you? Being too loud, too big, or "too much" is a common fear. But if we squash our biggest and brightest selves down all the time, we can't achieve our full potential. Popstars are so charismatic and flamboyant they're often called "larger than life". For someone so miniature, Ariana seems ten feet tall when she's performing onstage. Lots of popstars adopt an imaginary persona when they perform, to pump up the volume on their show. It's not fake—as Ariana says, it's an "exaggerated version" of her. If you have a big event you're nervous about, consider channeling the part of you that feels confident and outgoing.

"I've said this a million times: I hate drama.
I love women in the industry. I'm a big fan of
all my peers, and I try to keep it a hundred."

FOCUS ON YOU

Jealousy is a normal human emotion. We all occasionally feel that stab of envy when someone gets a fancy designer purse for their birthday or breaks our global streaming record. Doesn't it make you want to scream? Ariana works in perhaps the most competitive industry in the world: popstardom. We tend to feel most jealous of people who are actually similar to us and want similar things. You're more likely to feel jealous of the girl who sits next to you in class than the teacher. And there are so many ways for popstars to be compared: number of Grammys, number of records sold, biggest fandom. Additionally, the media is constantly on the lookout for a feud between famous women they can add fuel to. But Ari says "no". The solution, which Ariana demonstrates, is to stay calm and see people in competition with you as your peers, not your enemies.

66

The pony has gone through an evolution and I'm proud of that.

99

TURN SETBACKS INTO WINS

Truly famous celebrities can often be recognized from their silhouette alone—you could probably clock Ariana just from her shadow! Ariana's ponytail is the most famous and iconic element of her image. What you might not know is that the ponytail started out as an emergency solution to a beauty dilemma. When Ariana was playing Cat Valentine on *Victorious* and *Sam & Cat*, she had to bleach her hair and then dye it red. This caused so much damage that she started smoothing her real hair back and attaching a ponytail made of hair extensions. Although it started as a cover-up for her hair insecurities, the high ponytail turned out to be perfect for swishing and gave a unique element to Ariana's image. Over time, the ponytail has crept higher and lower on her head and been every color from chocolate brown to platinum blonde. When you're having a bad hair day, why not try the Ariana method and go for a dramatic change. You might even discover your own signature look.

"I've been open in my art and open in my DMs and my conversations with my fans directly, and I want to be there for them, so I share things that I think they'll find comfort in knowing that I go through as well."

SHARE YOUR FEELINGS

Being vulnerable is key for musicians like Ariana. She has to be able to share her life with fans through her music, forming a bond with us and maintaining that connection as we all grow. But as much as the word "vulnerability" is thrown around, it's not easy to maintain. It doesn't mean sharing every little thing, like we're still in the blogging era. It means being open and honest about what matters. But how do we continue to do that when it seems like everything gets picked apart online, or in Ari's case by the media? Ariana prioritizes connection with others. By sharing experiences with fans, she can show us that we're not alone in what we're going through. Part of putting out music is knowing that people will project their own experiences onto the songs and make them part of their own lives. It takes strength to be this open—Ariana was moved to tears as she described some of the songs on her 2024 album *Eternal Sunshine* as "really vulnerable".

"I learned how to make it sound like I was belting and being loud without actually belting and being loud. The voice is expensive, and if you're spending it properly, you'll be able to keep spending it."

WORK SMARTER

The only thing Ariana is more famous for than the ponytail is her voice. When you have a valuable instrument, you have to take care of it. Resting her voice and not overstretching herself is key. This is a useful lesson for every aspect of how we give our energy. We each have abilities and limits. Think of your energy, your kindness, your empathy, or your time as Ariana's singing voice. You might be the most amazing listener in the world, but this skill is "expensive" and you need to spend it properly. If you are exhausted from listening to one friend for hours on Monday, how will you be able to start all over again on Tuesday? Remember to take care of yourself and rest. If Ariana gave it all on night one of the tour, she'd have nothing left for the crowds at each subsequent date. It feels great to please her fans in Rio, but what about in London, Singapore, and New York? Being honest with yourself about your limitations can stop you burning out.

CHAPTER 5

BREAKING

FREE

So, you've read this far and you don't have the answers to life's big questions. Well, neither does Ariana. She's a work in progress, like all of us. She's ready to learn and transform in every stage of life. The most important thing is to stay open to change and take it easy on yourself. Sing the big notes, ask the big questions, and be more Ariana.

"This is the first album and also the first year of my life where I'm realizing that I can no longer put off spending time with myself [...] It was this scary moment of 'Wow, you have to face all this stuff now. No more distractions. You have to heal all this ****.'"

BE YOUR OWN BEST FRIEND

Being alone can be scary. Whether that means being single, ditching friends who aren't treating you well, or moving farther away from family, we all fear loneliness. Unfortunately, surrounding yourself with people isn't necessarily a cure for loneliness. Neither is filling our lives with calendar events or scrolling our phones endlessly to drown out pesky emotions. There comes a point when you have to become who you really are and live the life you really live. For Ariana, recording *Thank U, Next* showed that she could express her truest emotions and not overthink it. In the title song, she lists her exes and looks back on them fondly. The message of the song is not that she's looking for a new name for the list, but that her new boo is herself. Who was she without a Sean, Pete, or Malcolm? This was the moment she really became Ariana.

"I see myself onstage as this perfectly polished, great-at-my-job entertainer, and then [sometimes] I'm just this little basket-case puddle of figuring it out."

LET YOURSELF FLOP

Take Ariana's word for it—in a single day you can excel and feel like a total flop. She's a consummate performer who never misses a note and provides an incredible show no matter what. In that realm, she is perfectly poised and ready for anything. But professional success and immense talent doesn't mean she has everything figured out in her personal life. Does anyone? We'd all love to be perfect at new things on the first try. That includes big life stuff like relationships. It would be amazing if we found the perfect relationship the first time we fell in love and it lasted forever. But that's just not how life works: we need to test ourselves, make mistakes, and learn about ourselves. The big secret is that, no matter how confident those around you might seem, we are all "puddles of figuring it out" at love and life.

"Even at my most heartbroken or pained moments
of the past few years, there was so much kindness,
there was so much love, there was so much honesty,
transparency, and respect."

LOOK TO THE LIGHT

When you feel overwhelmed by sadness or really down on your luck, there are some practical self-help strategies you can try. Gratitude journaling actually works. If you've never tried it, it might sound too earnest. "What, I'm supposed to write down what I'm grateful for, even when I feel terrible?!" But somehow it does work, not because you don't have good reasons to be sad, but because it gives you a context for it. Ariana has been through some terrible times and surely has some very down days. But she continues to try and make sense of what she's been through and take action rather than staying in self-pity. Yes, she experienced the terrorist attack in Manchester, but she notices that people still have kindness in them. She has lost people, including her ex Mac Miller, but she observes that she still has people to love, who love her. Life is never 100% amazing or 100% bleak.

"I try not to catastrophize. I try to stay present. I think that a lot of our work as human beings is to not live in the past or in the future but to try and just be right here and focus on the present."

5, 4, 3, 2, 1

"Catastrophizing" is when you live in fear that the worst will happen. It's a serious symptom of anxiety that can end up really affecting your life. If you have severe anxious thoughts or panic attacks, it's important to find ways to focus on the here and now. Imagine you're Ari onstage. She has one clear job to do and it's to put on a live show, right now. When you're feeling severely anxious, your one job is to take care of yourself and stay in the present. This is not the time to dwell on the past or fixate on the future. If you feel panic symptoms coming on, try this technique for grounding yourself:

List 5 things you can see, 4 things you can touch, 3 things you can hear, 2 things you can smell, and 1 thing you can taste. Hopefully, by the time you reach taste you'll feel more centered and in the moment.

"Music needs to make people feel
hopeful and free and happy."

YOU DESERVE HAPPINESS

In this book, we've covered some of the best and worst moments in Ariana's life, from traumatic times to her glittering onstage performances. She is an actor, a fashion icon, and a role model for self-care, but most importantly she is one of the greatest popstars of all time. Ari channels hope, freedom, and joy into her performances, and it shines through in everything that she shares with the world. In every interview, Ariana comes across as sweet, thoughtful, and eager to do her best for her fans. Being inspired by Ariana means channelling breeziness and fun without indulging in toxic positivity. It means embracing the messiness of life and still trying your very best. Above all it means putting good things into this world, whether it's pop songs that brighten up the charts or the small, everyday kindnesses that we can all do to be more Ariana.

Editor Millie Acers
Designer Isabelle Merry
Senior Production Editor Jennifer Murray
Senior Production Controller Louise Minihane
Senior Acquisitions Editor Pete Jorgensen
Managing Art Editor Jo Connor
Managing Director Mark Searle

Written by Satu Hämeenaho-Fox
Cover and interior illustrations Nastka Drabot
Additional artwork Isabelle Merry

DK would like to thank Becca Pitt, Michael Bolat and Sharon Heron for their assistance and Caroline West for proofreading.

Quotations: **p.6** *Allure* (interview), 2017; **p.7** *Rolling Stone* (interview), 2014; **p.8** *Complex* (interview), 2013; **p.10** *Allure* (interview), 2017; **p.12** *Elle* (interview), 2018; **p.14** *Vogue* (interview), 2019; **p.18** *Vogue* (interview), 2019; **p.20** *Complex* (interview), 2013; **p.21** *Zach Sang* (video interview), 2024; **p.22** *Zach Sang* (video interview), 2019; **p.24** *Time* (interview), 2016; **p.25** *Billboard* (interview), 2016; **p.25** *Zach Sang* (video interview), 2024; **p.26** *Complex* (interview), 2013; **p.30** *ABC News* (interview), 2018; **p.32** *Elle* (interview), 2018; **p.34** *Fader* (interview), 2018; **p.36** *Elle* (interview), 2018; **p.38** *Vogue* (interview), 2019; **p.39** *Echo* (interview), 2017; **p.42** *Vogue* (interview), 2019; **p.44** *Billboard* (interview), 2016; **p.46** *Fader* (interview), 2018; **p.48** *Vogue* (interview), 2019; **p.49** *Instagram* (video), 2024; **p.50** *Vogue* (interview), 2019; **p.54** *Vogue* (interview), 2019; **p.56** *Vogue* (interview), 2019; **p.58** *Zach Sang* (video interview), 2024; **p.60** *Zane Lowe Apple Music* (video interview), 2024; **p.62** *British Vogue* (interview), 2018

First American Edition, 2025
Published in the United States by DK Publishing
1745 Broadway, 20th Floor, New York, NY 10019

Copyright © 2025 Dorling Kindersley Limited
DK, a Division of Penguin Random House LLC

25 26 27 28 29 10 9 8 7 6 5 4 3 2 1
001–345249–April/2025

Published in Great Britain by
Dorling Kindersley Limited

A catalog record for this book is available from the Library of Congress.
ISBN 978-0-5939-6160-5

DK books are available at special discounts when purchased in bulk for sales promotions, premiums, fund-raising, or educational use. For details, contact: DK Publishing Special Markets, 1745 Broadway, 20th Floor, New York, NY 10019
SpecialSales@dk.com

Printed and bound in China

www.dk.com